You Prayed for a Black Baby?

Marsha Johnson
You Prayed for a Black Baby?

All rights reserved
Copyright © 2024 by Marsha Johnson

Published by Spines
ISBN: 979-8-89569-641-5

You Prayed for a Black Baby?

THE STORIES OF FIVE EXTRAORDINARY BLACK WOMEN

MARSHA JOHNSON

Contents

You Prayed for a Black Baby?

The stories of five extraordinary black women.

The Extraordinary Ones!

There are two amazing women that I want to acknowledge and dedicate this book to, My mom Dr. Vara L. Mitchener & My cousin/auntie THE Mrs. Jacqueline Lacey.

This book is dedicated to my mother, the late Dr. Vara L. Mitchener affectionately known as Ms. Tudy. She's the one that started all this, praying for a "black baby". Mmmmmm Hmmmm that's right, she prayed and ask God for a black baby. I'm so grateful that she did and because of her prayer God sent me right to her.

I was blessed to be given to such an anointed, powerful, wise, giving and no nonsense woman that only God the Father knew could do the job and well. My siblings and I always say we had the best mother anyone could have asked for. Thank you for building me up when so many tried to tear me down, being my support system, my counselor, my biggest cheerleader my prayer warrior and foundation layer.

I am who I am in Christ and still growing because of the foundation you laid, and for that I will forever be grateful. I love you and miss you ma! I know you are resting right inthe bosom of Our Lord and Savior Jesus. Until we see each other again.

The next amazing woman that I would like to dedicate this book to is my cousin/auntie Mrs. Jacquline Lacey. What can I say about my cousin/auntie Jackie. Thank you for me doesn't seem to express my gratitude to you and how you played a major part in my confidence building along with my mom. You were a major reason why I looked forward to family reunions.

I knew when I saw you, you were going to greet me with that big ole gorgeous smile and some of the most beautiful chocolate skin and say, "Hey pretty girl"! I laugh because even now in both of our older ages, when we see each other, you still greet me the same. You always made me feel like the most beautiful black girl walking. I literally would feel different on the inside, like, yeah, I am beautiful. The color of my skin is beautiful, no matter what people may say about me. You are so smart, gorgeous and regal and I admire you so much cousin/auntie Jackie. And I THANK YOU! Your words and expression of love towards me every time I saw you made me stand a little taller and made me straighten my back. I am forever grateful to you, I love you!~ Marsha

The Extraordinary Ones!
What does it mean to be EXTRAORDINARY? When you look up the definition of the word EXTRAORDINARY you see descriptive words like, very great, tremendous, considerable and many other flattering and blushing words.
When I thought to use the word extraordinary to describe
myself and the other four women it was because not one of us is ordinary by any sense of the word. As you read each story starting with myself Marsha, LaChanda, Ebone', Quiandria and Dana you will see what I mean and why I chose the word EXTRAORDINARY.
I want to thank these you Extraordinary women for being brave and selfless in sharing your experiences, your heart your stories in all transparency. I know that because of your stories, many will find their voices and embrace who God has created them to be inside and out.
Without you all this project would never have come to fruition, so I want to thank you for your trust, patience and love!
It's been a long ride, but we made it!
From your sister, your friend and Ebone' your mom...
I appreciate you all and FOREVER LOVE!
~Marsha J.

Introduction

The five short stories in this book, are from five extraordinary women who just happened to be of darker skin. Each of our stories are unique, but at the core they are all similar. We all have dealt with the backlash of being a Dark-Skinned woman at some point in our lives. As you read each of our stories, I want you to allow yourself to go where we've been, feel what we've felt. You may have had some of your own experiences or maybe your mother, your sister, daughter, niece or sister-friend. Or you may have never experienced any form of racism, discrimination or colorism, if so consider it a blessing.

So as you read, I hope that you find healing or get a revelation that can help you get another person through who may have experienced the cruelty of others because of their skin color. This book is in no way to bash, bring separation or make anyone feel bad. I want to bring awareness, hope and change to the woman or man that's reading this book.

Learning, understanding and knowing that the color of your skin does not define who you are and were created to be.

That God Himself absolutely made no mistakes when He fashioned you. Remember, no one can define you because they didn't create you! Only Your creator can define you, because only He knows you better than you (Genesis 1:27).

My prayer is that you learn to love yourself, accept yourself, and embrace yourself and others who are different than you. Become compassionate to those who may be experiencing hurts that you can't see as a result of racism, colorism or discrimination. Find yourself while reading each story, and if there are unresolved issues and hurts from your present and or past that you confront and heal from them. Accept the skin you're in, YOUR skin! I hope by reading these stories, it will begin the conversation in our homes, communities and beyond.

You Prayed for a Black Baby?

JEREMIAH 1:5 (CJB)

"Before I formed you in the womb, I knew you; before you were born, I separated you for

Myself. I have appointed you to be a prophet to the nations".

People who know me now would have never thought that I was an insecure, angry, aggressive, verbally combative female that was always on guard and ready to fight, and fight I did. You couldn't mess with me, my sister or brother who are older by the way. Yes, that's right I'm the youngest of three and the darkest. Still am and always will be. I laugh as I'm sitting here typing out some of my life's journey, I can hear my mother's voice. My strawberry, vanilla and chocolate, that's what she called us. My sister Terra (Big Slim) who is the oldest was strawberry because of her complexion, my brother (JJ, he's chilling in the bosom of Jesus) he was vanilla and then there's me her chocolate baby, and in my opinion her favorite. No just kidding, my mom loved us all the same but different according to who we are.

When it came to me though, she would let me know that she had to do things a bit different because my skin was darker. I remember as a child there weren't too many pleasant encounters when I was around certain family members.

Like there was this one time we were at a family gathering of some sort, then again it may have just been us, the family over at my grandma's house like always. Well anyway, I walked in and my mom, a great-aunt, a family friend and my grandma. They were talking when I walked in, and I heard my great-aunt say to my mother, "you prayed for a black baby, why you pray for a black baby?" My mother's response was, "yes I did pray for a black baby!" Yep, you guessed it, ummm hmmm that "black baby" was me that they were speaking of.

Now this great-aunt, just so happened to be one of the many adults in my life that made sure I didn't forget that I was the black one. The slick comments every chance she got. She was of lighter skin, and somewhere in her mind that made her better I guess. Crazy thing is she had a DARK husband and a son who was just as DARK, Ha! I remember another time we were in North Carolina at a family reunion, we were outside in a yard. The picnic tables and chairs were placed all around the yard. I have a big family, so we were just doing what we do at a family reunion, running around playing you know kid stuff. Now, there were other instances where she would make comments about my skin color, and I would always tell my daddy.

Well, this time she made her comments about me being black. My feelings were so hurt, like all the other times. I couldn't wait to get back to D.C. so I could tell my daddy.

When we got back to D.C. and we got home, I told my daddy what she had said to me. I was still upset. I'll never forget, my daddy told my mother to tell that old lady "If she says one more thing to my child or about my child, Im'macuss her a** out!" My daddy was mad, and he meant it too, see my daddy mouth wasn't to right, at times, he would say whatever to whoever and didn't care. Apparently at some point my momma relayed the message, because the next time I saw her she didn't say anything to me but hi.

It didn't stop or start with my great-aunt. See, in my family talking "trash" about each other was a normal thing to do, especially amongst the cousins. It, was called joannin', older people call it playing the dozens. The entire purpose behind joanning, is to pick out a "flaw" of a person, and just drag it to the mud. It not only happened in my family, but at school and in my neighborhood. If you didn't have tough skin, or if you were just not feeling it on a particular day things could and would go way left. Because the whole object was to make sure that you out joanned the other person. So many times if not every time, someone walked away with their feelings hurt and they were mad because joanning was a daily occurrence.

Now for me, the joanning wasn't going to last too long before I was ready to fight. Yeah I joanned back, because that's what you did. It's a part of your defense, they say something bad about you, you say something worse about them.

But, it always became a serious problem when they would take shots at my skin color. Oh! I would get so mad and all bets and gloves were off! See, I dealt with it from not only family, but classmates, neighborhood kids, even people I didn't know would make comments. I felt the criticism, and backlash everyday all day which brought on several internal issues and struggles that I battled with for years as I continued to grow as a young black girl living in the nation's capital, you know the former "Chocolate City."

There are so many bad and sad memories that come into mind. I remember my first encounter with racism was at the age of five. When I attended an early childhood education school where my mom and one of my aunts were educators. This school was mixed with black and white children. This school was located on Capitol Hill in Washington, D.C.. The school is now a swanky gym facility. Thinking back I had friends that were not black and we were kids we didn't care, we were just kids. The friendship and love for each other was genuine. There were a set of twin brothers, they had blond hair and blue eyes and they wore the page boy hair cut style. They were my buddies. We played together every day at recess, at play time, lunch and snack time, we all sat at the same table.

Well if you haven't noticed by now, I'm Marsha. See Marsha is not really an "ethnic" name. So when the twins would go home they would talk about Marsha to their parents. They had talked me up so much, their parents couldn't wait to meet Marsha in their class. Now, keep in mind they didn't know that their son's teacher was also my mom who was my teacher as well. The day I met the twin's parents, we were excited. We were in the hallway of the school building.

One of the twins ran over to me grabbed my arm and pulled me while running so that I could meet their mom. As my mother and the twin's mother and father stood talking, we ran up on them as kids do and interrupted the conversation.

They were really excited to show their parents their friend Marsha. As I stood there with my neatly braided plaits with beads on the ends of my hair, I watched the face of the twins mother turn red and cold. Her smile faded as she looked upon me, towering over me and looking down at me in disappointment. In that moment, my mom became the superhero she was, and she pulled me to her side and said "this is Marsha, Marsha is also my youngest daughter." I don't remember a lot about what happened exactly after that moment, but what has and always will be etched in my mind, is the face of my friend's mother, that cold red and disappointed look she gave looking at a little black girl whom her sons loved so much.

As I moved on to grade school. The experiences became more frequent and worse. So much so that by the time I was in fifth and sixth grades I began to cut school. I just didn't want to deal with what became constant name calling. My mother's mother lived on the Capitol Hill side of the city, we lived on the other side of the city, and in an area called Congress Heights so I caught the metro bus across town to go to school. The times that I would ditch school, I would leave out like normal day, but I would go over to the laundry room and wait for everybody to leave then I'd go back in the house. During my sixth grade year, one day I had cut school one day too many, so they called my mom at work. I was scared for my life when my mother came home and told me the school called her, and said I wasn't at school and I had missed a few days and asked her was everything ok. I cried so bad, when I broke down and told my mother what had been going on and that's why I was skipping school. My mother was hot!

My mother called the principal and told her what had been happening to me, and that she wanted every child's parent to come to the school for a meeting. Two days later, when I arrived at the school with my mother. We had a meeting in the principal's office that had this large wooden conference table with more than half my classmates and their parents in the room sitting at the table.

We sat down across from everyone with the principal at the head of the table. My mother and the principal both told me to tell each parent what their child had said to me. I remember feeling terrified, sad and hurt.

Those kids called me black and blacky and said that I

was ugly because I was black. Things like "your father's sperm was bad and that's why you so black." And when I lashed out, they all conspired against me to jump me one day after school. So there I was telling these parents my mom and principal all the stuff my classmates said to me on a daily, with tears running down my face.

The scars that come from the abuse and wombs of childhood ridicule can last for decades and for some they never go away. The treatment of people, no matter who they are can be so instrumental and even detrimental to the self-esteem of an individual. It's hard enough being a woman, and then your skin color that almost from the day you are born, people see it as wrong ugly. And as we grow, it gets worse and worse starting with family, and then people in your own culture (colorism) and for the icing on the cake, racists America. You get hit from all sides with no days off. Literally at every stage of my life, I've had to deal with some form discrimination, separation or backlash because of the amount of melanin in my skin.

I was fortunate enough that I had parents that never made me feel like I was less than the best. Always boosting my confidence and in their own way, telling me and teaching me to own it. If you ask some, they may say they gave me too much confidence, Ha! But even with the confidence that I had learned to develop, there were still areas in me that were broken and looking for acceptance. Even though I knew what I knew and was told amazing things about myself and taught that I am the apple of God's eye and how I was fearfully and wonderfully made, all of those things and I spoke those things and in the moment I would feel great, like Yes! I got this! But when I wasn't around the people who loved and encouraged me, I often questioned if I really loved myself. After years of 'masking" I realized no, I didn't. The hardest part was admitting it.

The journey of self-love had to begin. As I became older, the thought of who I was wasn't really a front running thought. I just lived with it, never thought about it, until someone would make a comment or comments. Or, when being out you see how you're treated because you aren't the lighter skinned female. But see I am that dark skinned female that has made it a point in my life to never look "shabby". Never will my hair be undone, or I'm not dressed for the occasion (whatever it would be), I was just never not together. This has brought about issues for others, yes others because I'm good with me; or so I thought. The looks, the stares, the what I call stupid comments especially from men, like "oh, you're cute for a dark-skinned girl" really? Really?! What does that mean? I have asked many of guys that question and they either stumble over their words, or they remained silent. I'm over the age of forty now, and I still do not know what that means, "Oh you cute for a darkskinned girl".

Yeah, I know I know. I'm supposed to know what they mean. But, I don't! And no one has ever clarified it to me. See the way I interpret it as, because I'm of darker skin I'm not supposed to be "cute", I figure I'm supposed to look like a monster or something because I have more melanin in my skin? That's absurd! I remember when a female acquaintance who is brown-skinned, told me that because I was dark that my feet should be ugly. All I could do was shake my head, and the crazy part is, she's the one with bunions and corns on her feet. Now how crazy is that? Even though I would brush the comments off, they from time to time resurfaced in my thoughts. Especially when and if I heard of similar situations from other dark-skinned women.

These seeds that were planted into my psyche by others from my childhood and now adulthood really did begin to take root and grow. Well, the ones from my childhood were already there, so I guess the new seeds in adulthood just added to what was already planted. I carried this damaged, unaware woman into bad relationship after bad relationship. In my early twenties, I remember the first time myself and my ex-husband were doing open session counseling at the ministry that I attend. I raised my hand to ask my pastor a question. He acknowledged me and I proceeded to ask my question. My question was about how to allow my soon to be husband lead, when I was raised to be so strong, and I became this no nonsense woman. Also I was a single mom and I had become use to being this strong independent woman. How do I allow him to lead me? In that moment, it felt like it was just me and my pastor.

He proceeded to tell me that, though what was instilled in me and how I took and developed the woman that I had become I needed to first find out who God says I am. Not that what my parents had told me was wrong, but only the creator of someone or something can truly define it. In that moment I cried so hard. I remember feeling like the woman that I had developed into, I now have to give her up? I knew that this would make me vulnerable, I felt like I would become a weak woman but I knew it had to be done. So over a course of time, I began to change. Just as I felt it would happened, the worst thing. He began to notice and take my kindness (me softening up) for weakness. I tried to go along thinking that it was all in my head that the verbal and emotional abuse that began was just him exerting himself. I felt like, well maybe I didn't pay it any attention before because I would be abrasive and a take charge kind of woman. So needless to say the FIRST try was a no go.

After we split the first time, I became even more abrasive, verbally combative and on the defense when it came to any man that I felt was "doing me wrong". It wasn't until years later that I really discovered and acknowledged that I needed to change. I needed to get rid of the anger and hurt that stemmed from my past. It was hard because there were other relationships that ended horribly, because of cheating and lying and to add insult to injury the guy(s) would cheat with another females that would be a lot lighter than myself. So that didn't help with my esteem at all, even in my now adult age.

Throughout the years, a few more heart breaks and I allowing myself to be mistreated by people all while wearing a hard mask as if I wasn't phased by the way people treated me and talked to me. I had reached a place where I could no longer allow the meanest and hurt that others inflicted upon me keep me trapped. I had to do exactly what I learned when I was a child and then reiterated by my pastor. I had to first, forgive myself for taking on the views of how others saw me in their ignorance. Moving forward by truly embracing Marsha and the skin that I'm in. Knowing that the Creator God Himself made me this way, that yes I was fearfully and wonderfully made (Psalm 139:13-14 ESV). Created in His image and likeness (Genesis 1:27 KJV), knowing that I am truly the apple of God's eye I am His favorite. I had to renew my mind with positive affirmations, speaking life over myself seeing the beauty in this rich dark chocolate skin. Knowing that I come from greatness, great stock. That my skin and my roots run deep and the soil in which they were buried and have grown is rich.

Learning to love me and the skin that I'm in has been a journey. Crazy enough I'm still on that journey, learning more about me seeing how others are actually envious that they aren't me that they can't be like me. Cocky right? No, not even close. I've just learned in my little bit of living that there are many that hate me because of this permanent tan that I wear every day of my life. It's funny and sad all at the same time, because it's other people of color that has caused the most hurt to me because of what I look like. Something that I had absolutely no say in, and I'm glad God didn't ask me my opinion because I would not be the woman I am today. Now, I have experienced discrimination on all levels from many different races, even when traveling out of the country I've had my encounters of the racism. But the pain hits different when it's from people in your own race. Colorism is real! I always think when I have these encounters, like really? We are our own worst enemies. Either way I still press on in this chocolate casing that I've been blessed with.

As I sit here and write some of my story about my journey I've been on as a dark skinned woman. I've endured colorism, racism, judgment, criticism and even discrimination. Through it all I've managed to rise! Make no mistakes about it, I've been able to rise and bounce back every time because of who I am in God. Even when I didn't know or understand who I was fully in Him, He still pulled me up and pushed me along to this point in my life and He's still with me because my journey is far from over.

Yeah I know, sounds churchy and religious. But, I cannot, not acknowledge the very One who is behind my continual growth in self-love. Once I fully understood His love for me, that's when I began the process of truly loving myself. My self-esteem rose by leaps and bounds. When you see you how God sees you, you begin to change the narrative about who and what you are and were created to be and do regardless of what people have to say or feel about you, because it truly doesn't matter. Are some moments still challenging? Yes! But, I have to quickly remind myself of who I am when I'm faced with the mean and ignorant comments and stares from people of all races, yes even my "own" people. That's right, when I go to places, dinner, shopping and also church I get the same response. I've made it a point to walk with confidence no matter where I go and no matter how I feel.

I'm so grateful to my mom that she prayed for me, her "black baby." She started all of this with her prayers for me. She built me, and never broke me. She always would find ways and said things to remind me that this dark skin that I would forever be in was beautiful. I will be forever grateful to my mother for that, because now I wouldn't want to be any other skin tone than the one that I am DARK SKINNED!

The Blacker the Berry...

ONE COLD NOVEMBER DAY IN 1974, A seventeen-year-old girl gave birth to a Beautiful baby Girl. This young woman adored her new bundle of joy and thought she had the most beautiful dark skin. In fact, she was often complimented on how her babies dark skin was unique and special, little did she know, she was passing on to her years of ridicule and hardship. I'm sure that this young woman was totally unaware of the verbal and sometimes physical abuse that her daughter would endure. The young woman was totally oblivious to the harsh realities that her daughter would encounter growing up in SE DC in the 80's/90's.

During those times melanin was NOT in. It was considered a curse. In fact, it was a curse that plagued me the beautiful little dark skin baby) and a lot of other young girls that looked like me. For whatever reason, I always seem to stand out like a sore thumb. It didn't matter how nice I dressed or how good I smelled, I was the Girl that all the other kids felt it necessary to make feel like crap. For years, I was convinced that having dark skin was God's way of punishing me for whatever wrong that I may have done. My self- esteem was crushed. I was teased, bullied and humiliated all through school. I was called horrible names like blackie & African Booty Scratcher and the list goes on and on. When I became a teenager, things got worse, I developed the worst case of acne and my girlish figure refused to make herself known. I was never asked to any of the school dances and having a boyfriend was unthinkable. The guys that did show interest were adamant about keeping our relationship a secret (to avoid ridicule and shame).

There were so many lonely nights. When I went to the local teen events, I felt so alone. If it was a school dance, I stood in the background to ashamed to even attempt to get on the floor and let lose all of the latest dances. If it was the skating rink, I hid when it was couples skate because I knew that I would be looked over. I knew that it didn't matter that I was one of the best skaters or one of the best dancers, it didn't matter that I perfected these crafts because someone was sure to make it a point that I was this skinny black Girl who would never amount to anything and why not make fun of her. For most teens, life is about having a good time with friends and making lasting and incredible memories, for me, being a teen was exhausting. I found myself being overwhelmed with feelings of humiliation and self-hate. Allowing all that I had endured from previous years take complete control of my self-esteem. By the time I had entered my sophomore year in High school, I had become a pro at protecting myself from ignorant and hurtful comments. I found a way to cope. I found comedy. I realized that if I could talk about myself and make others laugh then that would save me the embarrassment of being let down by others.

When I was 15 yrs. Old I finally got my chance at courting. A guy in my 10th grade math class showed interest. I had no idea that my self-worth was at this point destroyed. All of the turmoil from previous years had made me toxic and I quickly ruined my chance at love. A year later, I got another chance to prove that I could be an excellent girlfriend. He and I hit it off great, we laughed and joked and really seemed to enjoy each other's company but it was all behind closed doors and I dare not share the news with my friends. Until I got pregnant my senior year of high school. When I shared the news of us becoming parents, he was more concerned with what others would say about him being with the ugly duckling. My parents thought that it would be best if I hid and not be the talk of the hood, so I was forced to move away and he was able to hide it all from the world.

Based on my parents theory, I would be much better off in another state little did any of us know that I would be treated like I was a victim of a heinous crime. I was taunted by numerous faculty in my new school. The principal made a comment that "I must have gotten pregnant in the dark". I was even told that my Baby would be "A little black monkey ". It was so bad that I was forced to have a full day of classes when I only needed 2 credits to graduate. Oh and the "little black monkey "was born the lightest baby in the nursery. After HS, I thought that things would finally get better. I thought that corporate America would be a little kinder and excepting. Much to my dismay, it was not.

Just when I started to love me for who God made me, just when I started to get the hang of being a Teenage Mom, corporate America placed a black cloud over my head like no other, but before I get to that you have to understand my mindset at 18 with a baby. I had decided long before my baby was born that I was going to get a college degree and nothing and no one was would get in my way, that is until the baby's father put his foot on my heart by continuing to feed my self-esteem with poison. I was made to feel like he was the only person who would accept me and that I would experience the same treatment in college.

At this point I was drowning in self-doubt but I had to provide. So with a High School diploma, I went to work. Ten years later, I was a mother of three and had been abused physically and mentally by both my baby father's along with being picked over by Big Executive companies. There reasons were one in the same, "it's not you, its use. We just don't need you. We have other candidates for the position. Only for me to find out later that a much fairer-skinned woman was there choice. It didn't matter that I was well qualified to be a great wife or a great employee.

That's when I turned to God. I was at the lowest point in my life, a time when I had no one else to turn to.

It was the best decision of my life. I began to see that I was fearfully and wondrously made. That my skin color did not define my character and that "The Blacker the Berry; The Sweeter the Juice". When I learned my self-worth and learned to put first, he blessed my abundantly with an AMAZING husband and a Career not just a job. I owe it all to The Most High. I am now ABSOLUTELY POSITIVE!! That I am a "Black Girl Who Rocks".

The Skin I Wished I Wasn't In

QUIANDRIA'S STORY

BLACKIE... BLACK... DARKNESS WERE JUST A few of the harsh words that I heard throughout my childhood. Mean and cruel words that pierced my heart and made me regret my existence. Why would I be born... dark skinned?

There's an old saying that goes "Sticks and stones may break my bones but words will never hurt." LIES! LIES! LIES! That saying is the biggest lie known to man! Some parents taught their children this rhythmic saying to combat bullies; it was a defense mechanism to shut down or counteract what was said. But, did it really make the victim of mean comments feel better, or did the words really hurt? My mom taught my sister and I that this was far from the truth; words do in fact hurt. Sticks and stones do have the potential of breaking our bones and leaving scars... But, words break beyond bones. You see, I've broken a bone before and it healed. However, there are moments where I still have to deal with "the words" spoken that broke my spirit. Not only do words hurt, but they take root. A wound will eventually become a scar, which may eventually fade away.

However, words can radiate and penetrate your heart leaving lasting effects...OUCH! Words have the power to shatter the foundation of your mind, heart and soul, leaving you buried in the sound effects of ridicule and low self-esteem. They are so powerful that it can shift your entire world. Harsh and mean words will play back repeatedly in your mind, like a record. If it's not uprooted, it will become embedded into your intellect, affecting and defecting your everyday life. The entire world was formed and fashioned based off words. God, the creator, said "Let there be" and it was. His words were so powerful that things that didn't exist manifested and became. The same power of words is prevalent today, whether good or bad, positive or negative, encouraging or chastising... words hold life or death.

I remember sitting in 9th grade Art class at a table amongst seniors. I was so excited to finally enter high school because it gave me a sense of feeling "grown up." When I learned of all the art classes that High School offered as electives, I was so excited! I had my brand-new sketch book for upcoming projects, my art supplies and my freshly printed syllabus. Let's not forget the fresh back-to-school outfit; I was ready! As I sat in my assigned seat according to my last name, I glimpsed around at the classroom in excitement, thinking "I'm in 9th grade... ready to bring exposure to my God given talent", until the chatter at my table started. It originated in subliminal comments that revolved around being black or dark. Honestly, it did take me a while to realize that these people were talking about me...the darkest kid at the table. What amazed me the most was as they teased and taunted me daily about my complexion, they still needed my help with art projects. They would ask me to help them draw various things. I figured if I helped them with the assignments that they couldn't do themselves, they'd stop making fun of me.

But, I was wrong; the torment continued. Third period - Art 1 became a place of torment! Each day they would tease and bully me for being "dark skinned" or in their words, "darky" or "blackie." I'm an artist and growing up, I loved to draw.

Unfortunately, the more I went to this "art" class, the more I hated art, my dark skin, the school and all of seniors sitting at the table. I absolutely dreaded going to art class... What I loved the most, Art class, became a place of devastation and horror! Hearing those painful things caused me to doubt that I was fearfully and wonderfully made. After all, why would God create me, knowing that I would be teased because of the shade He chose me to be? Why would they tease me when I didn't ask to be born in this outer shell that's a few shades darker than theirs? I hated the skin I was in! I wanted to be light skinned so bad, or at least a few shades lighter than what I was! I never shared with anyone what I was going through, I dealt with it alone.

I felt that men only wanted light-skinned women because being dark-skinned had such a horrible stigma. I felt this way until the day I met a guy (who happened to be light-skinned) that called me beautiful and loved my dark complexion.

Although our relationship didn't last, he helped me to see the beauty in my complexion. As years passed, I had other encounters when men would compliment my dark skin saying "I just love dark skin women... the blacker the berry the sweeter the juice". Even when it was a term of endearment, I still was affected and I used to cringe when someone said "dark-skinned" or "black" etc. even when no harm was meant.

In adulthood, various topics would arise and comments were made about complexion, almost as if we are two separate classes or entities. How did we get to this point of comparing complexions to decide which was better? Light skin vs. dark skin...Why is it a war? Can we consider this a "black on black crime" against one another? Could it be that we're racist against one another and don't even realize it? What if the World was color blind? All of this dates back to the Garden of Eden, before the fall and before Adam and Eve's eyes were opened. Now, we see everything and can easily find fault because our eyes have been opened to the wrong things. Instead of embracing and seeing beauty in all things, we see the wrong.

Don't get me wrong, I'm certain people who are light-skinned experienced the same issues and may have felt how I've felt. So, "no shade" to them (no pun intended). However, in most cases people made those who were light-skinned feel that they were superior or better. What would be the lesson in all of this? Why would The Lord allow me to experience something so painful that was beyond my control? When I was granted the opportunity to write an excerpt in this book, I was instructed by The Lord to write down the word "human" and to separate the "HU" and "MAN". In art class, we learned about hues, which mean both a color and a shade of a color. Most of the time the word hue refers to colors, but sometimes it's used for shades of meaning or even the tone of a person's face. This amazed me because it confirmed how intentional God is.

He purposely created "hu-mans" with different "hues" "shades" and "colors" to demonstrate His wonder! He mixed different shades of color, personality, DNA and much more to create us ALL, in HIS image. It was in my time of reflection and preparation to write this excerpt that I realized and fully grasped that God is the Master Creator. He created and fashioned me the way He desired; height...weight...personality and COMPLEXION on purpose and with a purpose. He had me in mind the entire time.

When God decides to send us into the World, we have no clue what family we'd be born into, what we'd look like or who we'd grow up to be... The only instruction was to get here and He would handle the rest.

It took me many years to embrace my dark skin and not be offended by comments like "the dark-skinned girl"... To be honest, I'm still making strides to embrace how God "painted" me. I've embraced my dark skin... Will you?

My Blessing is Being a Black Girl

EBONE'S STORY

Growing up with deeper colored skin has by far been the most challenging part about existing in this world. It saddens me that in every aspect of life that what color shade your skin is whether it's in the work-force, entertainment business, beauty industry, model-ing, etc.. It can be the determining factor of one's success. Throughout my childhood, I was bullied because of how dark my complexion is. All through grade school, all the comments came my way about being a dark-skinned girl. It all started when my mom first put me in school that's when the name-calling began and kids that looked just like me some being a few shades lighter than me replacing my name by degrading me as if I were not a human being. I've been called every name in the book there is. Picked-on and teased by someone whose skin was lighter than mine and some who were the same shade as me or darker. There were times those kids would ask me have I been PICKING COTTON all my life because of how dark my skin is. It made me so angry because it's not like I went to a predominantly white school, and it was white kids being racist. NO! It was my own community making a mockery of what our ancestors endured and using it as a joke to degrade me as not only a person of color but a human being. The amount of disgust I felt by the black community was beyond me.

Every day I went into each of my classes and took all of the bashings from kids who were of the same race as me. Tearing me down and every time I would stand up for myself, I got told by my teachers to "calm down" or "this is your warning before I have you step out of my class." Those types of comments made my blood boil. Because not only did the teachers that looked just like me, never took any actions to completely correct the kids that chose to disrespect me every chance they got. But I got told to "calm down," and the kids got told to stop. Like what was that?! NO ONE EVER CAME TO MY DEFENSE when I was in school. What type of young black girl every day has to go through such humiliation every single day for an entire school year and more years to come of being in school. I'll tell you a strong one. During that time, I didn't know that I was. All the boys would go for the girls who were popular and had lighter skin than mine. All the lighter-skinned girls had long straight or curly hair with the "baby hairs." I envied them because I'm thinking about the boys who would make fun of me and praised the girls who they felt "looked better" than me. Crazy enough, those girls were always loud and wanted attention. And my friends that were lighter than me the boys would always want to talk to them instead of me. See I was the one everyone would want to be cool with, but no one wanted to date me. Whenever a new girl came to my middle school, and if she were light-skinned, the boys would give her all the attention. A couple of boys have told me that they would want to date me if my skin were a few shades lighter, but it wasn't so they'd rather that we be just "friends." I hated middle school because of waking up every morning to go to school; I just felt invisible, and like I didn't matter.

I remember being in the 8th grade and a boy darker than me decided he wanted to joke about me having dark skin by calling me names. Everyone that was sitting in the back of the class with us laughed like I was the topic of the day and right then and there I began to cry. Everyone, I thought I was cool with was going along with him making jokes and laughing. At that moment I saw all of them as my enemies, I walked out of the class without asking for permission and went straight to the principal's (who is white) office to tell him what happened and asked could I call my mom because I wanted to go home. I couldn't stop crying; I was beyond angry and humiliated. My principal was a white man, and I felt he couldn't understand what I was going through because he wasn't black. Even if he was, he couldn't have fathomed the wrath I felt. No one in a position of authority in that school ever used their authority to put those kids in their place. They would bully me every single day and every chance they got. So I called my mom, and even though she did her best to calm me down, it wasn't good enough because she wasn't there to comfort me. The only action my principal took was to make the boy apologize, and for me, that wasn't good enough. I was so tired of the not-so-sorry apologies that those kids were made to give. Knowing that he didn't mean it, and knowing that he was going to do it again. My school, like many others fighting, wasn't allowed, which made me beyond mad because I wanted to punch that boy so bad. I began to keep a list of every person who ever bullied me every day, even the people outside of school. There were nights I had dreams of killing every single one of them but also making them feel my pain right before I would take their lives. That's how disgusted I felt. When we allow anger and rage to take over, it takes over. When being bullied all of my young age, there was no confidence in me; I didn't even know what confidence looked like because I was constantly ridiculed for the color of my skin. The hate I encountered every day all because of how dark my complexion is, shattered me, my spirit. Even though my mom did her best to instill confidence in me and letting me know how beautiful I was all the time, I didn't believe it. By the time high school came around, I had become accustomed to being overlooked and being in the shadows of all the light-skinned pretty girls all the boys gagged over. It became my new normal, but one thing changed in me, and it was my mouth. Once I knew the power of hurting someone with cruel words that was my way of trying to take back my power because I couldn't physically fight in school, so my mouth became my weapon. Yes, I got in trouble because of my mouth, but I didn't care because I felt no one ever cared or acknowledged how those bullies who used their words to hurt me. But with fighting back, I still felt ugly on the inside and outside and felt like one was there to have my back.

It's nothing like feeling completely alone and feeling like you don't belong inside a room with people who are also black. So once I got my first love in high school, it was very unexpected and interesting at the same time because I didn't believe that I would ever get a boyfriend and be friends with that person all the same time. He loved my dark skin, and that was a bonus because I was always the one being asked can I tell my light-skinned friend that a boy liked her.

It was refreshing but challenging because I had put up this wall so one else could hurt me and he had tried so hard to get me to let down my walls. Because he made me feel comfortable with just being me, so it made me feel safe to let down my guard. I felt for the first time I had someone truly liking me, and that felt good but also scary at the same time. He was the quarterback of our high school and the fact that he chose me knowing that he had so many other options; it made me feel like I was the "it" girl. I thought he'd be interested in a loudmouth popular light-skinned or brown-skinned girl, and on top of that he was a senior, and I was a sophomore. Within the three months of getting to know each other, we started dating, and we were together two years. He told me that he never dated a "chocolate" girl before and that it was refreshing to find someone that was pretty, chocolate low key. See while listening to him saying those things I automatically became defensive but as the conversation got deeper, I just said: "maybe you haven't been looking that close or even paying attention. It's millions of us dark-skinned girls that are beautiful." As we came into an agreement looking back, I notice that I was trying to make him complete me while being together. I was not whole before I had decided to be in a relationship.

All of my insecurities started to re-surface because I was looking for him to complete parts of me that only God could make whole. I never received that type of love from anyone outside of family. Having someone look at me and like me for the person I was, I wasn't use to that. Not feeling valued as a black teenaged girl in high school and my community and half my life, I was so used to hearing and being criticized by others and their negative opinions about my skin complexion. I had to apologize to him because it wasn't his job to fix me, and it was wrong of me to put that type of pressure on him to try and do so. I wanted to be seen by someone and for them to see me as a person and not just my dark skin. So for the rest of my high school years and in life I began to build my confidence, not through my ex but starting with me telling myself that I am worth every ounce of love, joy, and acknowledgments that came my way. I vowed not to let another person take or break who I am as a human being. I began to accept my dark skin and live. But all that strength wasn't built overnight; it took for me to believe it in my heart and start wearing that confidence every time I stepped out of the house.

When it came to certain people in my own family that would try to humiliate me by talking about my skin color, I didn't know how to feel because, after a while, it became such a blur. I heard all the comments before while being in school, and now I defend myself when they choose to comment and then walk away. I choose not to surround myself with them because I don't believe in being around ignorant people who come from the same bloodline and background as me. So I choose not to deal with them.

What I find truly interesting is that in the last few years people have jumped on this wave of embracing women of darker skin color. People everywhere family, friends, strangers everybody. It has kind of made me mad because for me it's not a trend or a statement piece that we wear to make ourselves look cool enough to be around or wear. Millions of other darker-skinned woman and I live with our complexion every day. It seems nowadays everyone wants to embrace the darker skin tone, and NOW they want all this "good melanin" as if it were ever bad or not good. The term "the blacker the berry, the sweeter the juice" seems to have made a comeback.

Either way, it doesn't change the fact that darker-skinned black women are still the most disrespected, and we still face daily challenges because of it. See I never loved myself enough the way I do now because I have allowed others insecurities channel the way I look at myself. But now that I am a young woman, no one's words or actions can break me as a black woman because I know that my dark skin is my story, it's who I am. For every young black queen, and any young woman of any race that may be reading my story, I want you to know that "Your magic is wrapped in flesh, Do not alter the layers of gold tucked in." You are unique, and You are Beautiful!

Badge of Honor

I had heard most of my life, "You're pretty for a dark- skinned girl" or "I would never have considered dating a dark-skinned black woman before I met you!" I wore these "compliments" like a badge of honor...

Growing up a military brat, color was never an issue or topic of discussion. In fact, we embraced the different ethnic backgrounds and cultures. Visiting other countries and states, most times I was accepted and almost praised for being "black". My mother (who also happens to be my shero) is a 22-year veteran whose complexion is darker than mine.

Her hands and feet are a beautiful shade of dark brown skin. Her smile is as white and wide as the sun. I lived with a BLACK BEAUTY! My grandmother was a bronze Goddess while my aunts and cousins were every shade from the natural hue and OWNING IT!

My first taste of hate towards the color of my skin was in Savannah, Georgia by an older white man. I was walking through a senior living complex near my house, when this man shouted out something like, "You black nigger, you need to get off this property!" In shock and fear, I ran home and told my aunt. She returned with me to that neighborhood to confront this man. He yelled out at her, "You fat black b!*$#.....!" My aunt realized that the man was beyond hope or reason and took us back home.

In the seventh grade living in Washington state, a white boy, about the same age as me, told me to "go pick some cotton" while riding the bus home from school. I told my mother about it and she asked me who told me that. Then she explained to me that it was a racial slur and said that perhaps the little boy had racist parents for him to know to say that. Before these two incidents, I never knew there was an issue with the color of my skin. Glory be to God that I did not allow the ignorance of others to persuade me differently.

When guys would approach and go out dates with me, it never failed how I would change their opinion of darker-skinned black women. They would always compliment me on how pretty my skin and hair was! I was honored to bring such a positive light to my fellow colored sistas! "My momma always called me a "pretty black little girl" was what I told them. They assumed upon meeting me that I was stuck up or had a nasty attitude. However, after getting to know me through conversation they found that neither was applicable! I was a 6 ft., 300+ lbs. of pure milk chocolate ROYALTY! I carried (and still carry) myself like a QUEEN!

I was raised by a Nubian SOLDIER who taught me to be strong, tough, bold and BEAUTIFUL! I was taught to love my "black" skin. Due to that confidence, I can fix any woman's crown without worrying if it will diminish mine. I never knew there was dissension between women of color, but I'm glad to be a part of the conversation to bridge the gap! And now, being married to an African King and raising two princes of my own, we are intentional about making this skin look good! It is our BADGE OF HONOR!

Be Empowered!

Now that you have read each one of our stories, where are you in your life right now? Have you grown to be a confident individual who now embraces herself? Or are you still struggling with self-love because of the hurt you've experienced from your past, or maybe even present? Regardless of where you are in your process know this, You are more than enough! You were created to be EXACTLY who you are. You are loved, wanted, needed. You are special, unique and worthy. Yes, the stories you just read were from darker-skinned women, but that does not exclude you from still identifying and owning the skin you're in. Whether dark, light, or brown skinned you are special!

I chose just to put a few Encouraging quotes from some amazing women of color. Also listed are some scripture references to help you along if you're struggling with your identity, self-esteem and confidence. Read the quotes and scriptures aloud, so that you can hear yourself. That's right, you'll be speaking life over yourself, encouraging yourself and the more you do it the more you will internalize it and the more real it will become to you. And in that you'll see just how special, unique and wonderfully made you are.

Quotes & Scriptures...
"Whatever we believe about ourselves and ability comes true for us."

~ Susan L. Taylor

"Sometimes, I feel discriminated against, but it doesn't make me angry.
It merely astonishes me. How can any deny themselves the pleasure of my company? It's beyond me."

~ Zora Neal Hurston

Feeling rejected? You belong to God. **Isaiah 43:1**
Feeling alone? He is with you wherever you go. **Joshua 1:9**
When you feel or say I am weak, God says He's made you strong. **Psalm 18:32**
Feeling Worthless? You are Worth it! **John 3:16**
Feeling Unhappy? **John 15:11**
When you feel broken, God says I've made you whole.
Colossians 2:10
Feeling Hopeless? **Jeremiah 29:11**
Not Feeling Special? **Psalm 139:14**
Feeling like you have no purpose? **Esther 4:14**

I Am The Black Child

I am special, ridicule cannot sway me

I am strong, obstacles cannot stop me

I hold my head high, proudly proclaiming
my uniqueness

I hold my pace, continuing forward through
adversity

I am proud of my culture and my heritage

I am confident that I can achieve my every
goal

I am becoming all that I can be

I am the black child, I am a child of God

-Mychal Wynn